How Three Rivers

Connecticut, Hudson, and Delaware

Revolutionized Transportation,
Travel and Trade in America

by
John Bernardo

HERITAGE BOOKS
2019

HERITAGE BOOKS
AN IMPRINT OF HERITAGE BOOKS, INC.

Books, CDs, and more—Worldwide

For our listing of thousands of titles see our website at
www.HeritageBooks.com

Published 2019 by
HERITAGE BOOKS, INC.
Publishing Division
5810 Ruatan Street
Berwyn Heights, Md. 20740

Copyright © 2019 John Bernardo

Heritage Books by the author:
Hudson River: A Scenic and Historic Natural Treasure
Delaware River: America's Historic, Scenic, and Working Waterway
How Three Rivers (Connecticut, Hudson, and Delaware) Revolutionized Transportation, Travel and Trade in America

Cover photo (top): Steamship *Hendrick Hudson* on the Hudson River. This image is courtesy of the Historical Society of Rockland County in New City, New York.

Cover photo (bottom): *Onrust* is a replica of the first western style, sailing ships built in the New World and the first ever to sail up the Connecticut River. This image is courtesy of the Connecticut River Museum in Essex, Connecticut.

All rights reserved. No part of this book may be reproduced or transmitted in any form or by any means, electronic or mechanical, including photocopying, recording or by any information storage and retrieval system without written permission from the author, except for the inclusion of brief quotations in a review.

International Standard Book Numbers
Paperbound: 978-0-7884-5874-3

Table of Contents

Preface   v

     Introduction to Author and Book

Chapter 1:   1

     History of Connecticut River Boats with U.S. Waterborne Transportation, Travel and Trade

Chapter 2:   12

     History of Connecticut River's Shipbuilding/Trade Towns

Chapter 3:   18

     History of Hudson River Boats with U.S. Waterborne Transportation, Travel and Trade

Chapter 4:   37

     History of Hudson River's Shipbuilding/Trade Towns

Chapter 5:   43

     History of Delaware River Boats with U.S. Waterborne Transportation, Travel and Trade

Chapter 6:   49

     History of Delaware River's Shipbuilding/Trade Towns

Chapter 7: 60

    Canals That Improved Navigation for Vessels Transporting Commerce and Passengers on Connecticut, Hudson, and Delaware Rivers

Chapter 8: 72

    Today's Boats Navigating the Connecticut, Hudson, and Delaware Rivers

Author's Summary: 85

Preface

John Bernardo – How Three Rivers (Connecticut, Hudson, and Delaware) Revolutionized Transportation, Travel and Trade in America

Writing has been my passion since 1988 and so far I have written over 500 articles. Most of those stories were published in newspapers and some in magazines. In addition to my articles, I am now the published author of six books. My last book was about the Delaware River, which was published in July 2016.

Prior to my work regarding the Delaware River, I wrote a book on the Hudson River (published in 2013), another was a fiction book called *The River* (published in 2003). Before *The River* (published in July 2003), I was co-author of a book titled: *Airline Safety: The Passenger's Role* (published in April 2003) and then in July 2001 I became the published author of a book titled: *What You Can Do For Your Own Flying Safety and Security*.

I was motivated to write a book about the significant roles of commercial and passenger vessels on the Connecticut, Hudson, and Delaware Rivers regarding our nation's trade and transportation industries because I had already written books about the Delaware River and Hudson River.

And the information I gathered in the two books I just mentioned touched on commercial and recreational boats on the two rivers and how that enhanced our local and national economy. My books, *Delaware River* and *Hudson River*, also focused on how these waterways impacted trade in America and there are pictures of different vessels in those two books.

So in light of what I just mentioned I wanted to combine the Delaware River and the Hudson River in one book because of their role with our nation's waterborne transportation and trade system. As for the Connecticut River, I happened to pass by it a few years ago on my way to Rhode Island. After I passed the river I wondered what impact it had our nation's transportation system so I decided to research its role in our waterborne transportation industry.

Low and behold, through my research, I discovered that in addition to the Delaware and Hudson Rivers, the Connecticut had and still has an important impact on America's trade and transportation system. After I obtained information on the Connecticut River that was related to that of the Delaware and Hudson Rivers, I decided to add information about the Connecticut to my book. I also decided to include the Connecticut River in my work because, like the Delaware and Hudson, it flows within the Northeastern portion of America.

My book flows like a river from north to south. As you read it you'll see it focuses first on shipyards and vessels on the Connecticut, next I focus on the Hudson and then on the Delaware. Also any information that applies to two or three of the rivers will be included. Finally, you will see a variety of photos of shipyards and other images of ships of today and historic vessels that are navigating or once navigated the Connecticut, Hudson, and Delaware Rivers.

Chapter 1

History of Connecticut River Boats with U.S. Waterborne Transportation, Travel and Trade

Since the early 17th century, sailboats were under the direction of explorers that were discovering shorelines and waters of the Connecticut River. In fact, one sailing boat named "Onrust" was a Dutch Ship constructed by voyager Adriaen Block and his crew. Onrust was built in upstate New York in the winter of 1614 and was about 45 feet long and had a load capacity of 16 tons.

Onrust was launched in April 1614 and the vessel searched the New York shore and rivers (including the Hudson River). She then explored the ports of Long Island, New York and Connecticut and navigated up the Connecticut River past a location that is now known as Hartford, Connecticut. Historians also indicated that the last chronological account of Onrust outlines her 1616 journey to explore the Delaware River.

Also during the mid-1600s Onrust first began operating on the Connecticut River and found some of the region's ports, three towns in Connecticut along the Connecticut River, specifically Hartford, Middletown, and Glastonbury, represented the area's biggest harbors until the 1700s. In fact up until the 1840s, Hartford was the farthest upriver port accessible to deep draft sailing ships. And the three ports I just mentioned were heavily involved in trade where the boats that departed from these harbors shipped a lot of livestock, cheese, potatoes, corn, wheat and butter to the West Indies. In return, the vessels transported molasses and rum back to Connecticut.

Thanks to the three huge ports that I just mentioned, sailing boats in the 1700s and later steamship traffic during the 1800s increased on the Connecticut by around 1815. Also during the 19th century, daily steamer service between Hartford and New York City continued on the Connecticut River until 1931.

In fact, digressing to the 1800s, a huge system of canals and dams opened the river to flatboat and steamship traffic for over half the Connecticut River's length encouraging trade and travel. Furthermore, researchers and historians indicated that the Connecticut River was the first river in the United States to be altered for a significant distance for transportation. By the time construction began for the Erie Canal in 1817, several canals on the Connecticut already had opened it to riverboat traffic (flatboats and ocean-going vessels) from Long Island Sound to as far north as Hartford, Connecticut, which was the transfer point between ocean-running ships and smaller vessels that navigated the upper river.

Yet besides canals that were crucial to riverboat traffic regarding trade and travel on the Connecticut River, log drives on the Connecticut uplifted the region's economy beginning in the late 19th-century.

Hence, every spring from 1870 to 1915, crews on rafts drove more than a quarter of a million spruce logs down the river, from its headwaters in Quebec, Canada to sawmills in Massachusetts. The log drive on the Connecticut River was critical in delivering lumber needed to build many 19th-century New England cities.

Digressing from log drives to ferry boats, early passenger ferries on the Connecticut were actually rowboats and have operated on the river since the 17th-century. One ferry in particular, Bissell's Ferry, began to ply the river in 1648. The ferry service is not operating today but according to historical records, Bissell's Ferry, which connected Windsor, north of Hartford, Connecticut, was the oldest ferry in America. Another old ferry on the

Connecticut is the Rocky Hill-Glastonbury Ferry; in 1655, it started service as a small raft that pushed across the river using long poles. Then decades later, a horse on a treadmill in the middle of the boat provided the power to propel the vessel across the Connecticut River between Rocky Hill and Glastonbury, two towns in Connecticut.

Another ferryboat that started cruising the Connecticut was the Chester-Hadlyme Ferry, which began cruising the Connecticut River in 1769. The ferry was frequently used through the Revolutionary War to carry essential supplies across the river.

The original ferry was pushed across the river using long poles. Then during the late 1800s, a steam-powered barge started to serve the ferry crossing in 1879. The ferry was named Chester-Hadlyme in 1882 while it was operated by the Town of Chester, Connecticut. By 1917, ownership of the ferry was turned over to the Connecticut Department of Transportation.

In addition to passenger ferry service on the Connecticut River during the 17th and 18th centuries, ferries were used for trade. One example of a trade ferry was Tryall, then a small trade vessel. Constructed in 1649, Tryall navigated out of the Connecticut River loaded with timber and fresh farm produce. Tryall also marked the start of a prosperous trade developed between the state of Connecticut and the islands of West Indies.

Moving forward to the 18th-century, by 1700 the Connecticut had 11 ferry crossings and by 1750, the number of ferryboats increased to 26. Case in point, the Middletown Ferry had been in operation on the Connecticut River since 1727 and transported people to and from Middletown, Connecticut (later to other Conn. towns such as Portland, East Hampton, and parts of Middle Haddam). Then later in 1769, the Chester-Hadlyme Ferry began passenger service and connected King's Highway in Fort Hill, Parish of Chester to Norwich Road in Lyme, Connecticut. This ferryboat was also used frequently during the Revolutionary War to carry crucial supplies across the river.

At the end of the 1700's, 30 ferries navigated on different portions of the Connecticut River. Within the same period in 1776, a ship named "Oliver Cromwell" was built in a harbor in Essex, Connecticut. Historians claim that Oliver Cromwell was the first ship funded and commissioned by the Colony of Connecticut. She was also the biggest full-rigged vessel launched on the Connecticut River up until that period. Back then this ship was created so she could fight against the British during the Revolutionary War (1775 to 1783).

Also during that same era in 1793, inventor Samuel Morey of Orford, New Hampshire, operated his steamboat, "Aunt Sally," on the Connecticut River near Orford. One feature of Morey's boat is that it came with a side paddle wheel and Aunt Sally also was the first boat powered by an internal combustion engine.

Although Morey already demonstrated his steamer on the Connecticut River in 1793, historians claim that in 1810, was when the steamship, the "Fulton," moving at about four miles an hour, actually navigated up the Connecticut and was the first vessel to provide passenger service. In 1813, the Fulton started to transport people between two popular Connecticut towns, Hartford and Middletown, and in 1815, the steamer began passenger service between New York City and New Haven, Conn.

After steamboats Aunt Sally and Fulton made their appearances on the river, several steamships after 1815 plied the lower Connecticut River and many of these huge vessels made regular trips between Hartford, Conn. and New York City. By 1821, the number of ferries on the Connecticut fell to 20 yet nevertheless, that number remained the same for the next 50 years and the 19th-century marked the era for large sailing ships and steamboats.

Digressing to steamboats, the first steamboat appeared on the Connecticut River in 1822, running along the state of Connecticut from Hartford to Saybrook. Then in 1824, another steamship, "Oliver Ellsworth," started passenger service between

Hartford, Connecticut and New York City. Oliver Ellsworth was made by the Connecticut Steamboat Company, weighed almost 230 tons, and was 112 feet long. She was the first steam-powered, floating palace that navigated the river for the next 50 years. Oliver Ellsworth could transport up to 400 passengers and made three trips a week between Hartford and New York. At an average speed of eight knots, the Ellsworth ship could make the 140-mile voyage from Hartford to New York City in about eighteen hours.

In addition to Oliver Ellsworth, Barnet, a 75-foot-long steamship, was launched on the Connecticut River in 1826 when she arrived in Springfield, Massachusetts. During that same year, her maiden journey was successful and Barnet was the first steamship to navigate on the Connecticut River above Hartford, Connecticut despite the Enfield rapids. Barnet's successful run also had an important role in the Industrial Revolution and that led to huge commercial growth in Springfield and Hartford. However, her success didn't last long because in 1830, the state of Massachusetts granted charters to railway companies to build rail lines out of Boston that negatively affected the local steamship lines.

Yet despite railroads gaining with commercial and passenger transportation in New England, the number of steamboats on the Connecticut River increased tremendously after 1840. River traffic was then at its peak and three steamboat lines provided passenger service to New York. In 1846, there were more than 2,000 arrivals and departures of steam and sail vessels at Hartford's twenty-odd wharves despite that the city's population was only about 13,000.

Speaking of steam and sailboats, according to researchers and historians, the first steam ferry to navigate the Connecticut River was named the Mattabesset. Constructed in 1852, this vessel traveled up and down the Connecticut until 1889. Nevertheless, from the 1840s to 1850s, most ferry boats still operating on the river already converted into steamships.

As for steamboat service on the Connecticut River, even during the 1860s, steamboat travel from Hartford to Old Saybrook, Conn. was slow and took most of the day. Yet even though the speed of steamships was not that fast, stops continued to be made for freight and passengers at many towns in Connecticut along the Connecticut River including Middletown, East Haddam, Deep River and Essex.

In the 19th century, there were two screw-powered steamers called Hartford traveling on the Connecticut River. First there was a popular steamboat called "The City of Hartford," a 273-feet-long, white oak/chestnut colored steamer constructed in 1852. This steamer had 35 furnished staterooms and could transport up to 977 passengers. Since 1852, The City of Hartford served passengers on the Connecticut River for many years until the federal government acquired her for use as a transport ship during the Spanish-American War (April 1898 to August 1898).

In addition to the City of Hartford, in 1899, another steamer simply called Hartford was launched. Made by Columbia Iron Works and Dry Dock Company of Baltimore, Hartford was a gigantic, 244-feet-long, ship that weighed almost 1,500 tons, provided guests with over 60 private staterooms, and held over 300 passengers. This vessel also made stops at riverside communities in Connecticut such as Rocky Hill, Middle Haddam and Essex. The Hartford provided passenger service on the Connecticut River until 1938. Yet besides the Hartford steamers, starting from the Victorian Period (1837 to 1901) up to the early 1900s, luxurious side-wheelers and screw-powered steamboats were commonly seen on the Connecticut River.

ROCKY HILL HISTORICAL SOCIETY.

PHOTO NO. 0477,A,B.   GROUP 14

DATE--January 1925.

DESCRIPTION-

0477B-Ice breaker tug and excursion boat "Hartford" photographed together with people on the River watching them. East view.

Steamboat *Hartford* being followed by ice breaker on the Connecticut River, 1920s

Courtesy of the town of Rocky Hill, Connecticut

The *Rocky Hill Ferry* photographed on the Rocky Hill
side of the Connecticut River, 1900s

Courtesy of the town of Rocky Hill, Connecticut

Steamer *Middleton* on the Connecticut River
Courtesy of the Middlesex County Historical Society
in Middletown, Connecticut

Two-masted schooner on the Connecticut River
Courtesy of the Middlesex County Historical Society
in Middletown, Connecticut

Painting of Steamship *Oliver Cromwell* by Richard Brooks
Courtesy of the Connecticut River Museum
in Essex, Connecticut

Chapter 2

History of Connecticut River's Shipbuilding/Trade Towns

Since the 1600s, there were many towns in Connecticut on the Connecticut River that made a variety of ships that enhanced the transportation of freight and passengers on the Connecticut River. These shipbuilding river towns also improved the economy along the river, across New England, throughout the U.S., and across the world. But the Connecticut towns on the Connecticut River that I will focus on include Middletown, Essex, Haddam, Old Saybrook, Wethersfield, and Rocky Hill.

First there is Middletown, Conn., a city that was named for its location midway between the early settlements at Hartford and Saybrook. And since the 1660s, shipyards in Middletown were constantly making sailing vessels and that helped merchants in Middletown establish trade with ports along the East Coast, the West Indies, and Europe. Trade was one contributor to the town's growth and that's why in 1726, a small ferryboat started to provide people with regular crossings to and from Middletown.

By 1815, steamships began navigating the Connecticut River near Middletown. In fact in 1822, William Redfield, who is from Middletown, piloted his side-wheel steamer between Hartford, Conn. and New York City and stopped in Middletown on the way. For more than one hundred years, steam-powered vessels transported cargo and passengers in and out of Middletown and that motivated local factories to ship their commerce all over the globe.

Besides Middletown, another important riverboat building town on the Connecticut that needs to be mentioned is the town of Essex.

Essex has a long history of constructing ships; in fact, the town first started building vessels in 1733. During the 18th century and up to the 19th century, shipyards were abundant in Essex and for many years the town made many schooners (ships with two or more masts), packet ships (boats that travel regular routes carrying passengers, freight, and mail), sloops (sailing vessels having one mast), and other vessels used primarily in foreign trade. Back then, many men from the Essex community became seamen and sailed all over the globe on voyages that lasted several months.

During the late 1700s to early 1800s, Essex was a rich town. Its two deep coves located on both sides of the Essex Village Center provided a lot of space for shipbuilding. But unfortunately during the War of 1812, the British destroyed many warships manufactured in Essex and it slowed down the town's manufacturing base.

And in addition to the War of 1812 and well into the 19th century, wooden sailboat manufacturing plummeted as steamboat travel continued to blossom. Then in the 1820s, the first wooden steamboats on the Connecticut River began transporting passengers between Hartford and New York City. Hence, as demand for steamships continued to grow, shipwrights in Essex met that demand by constructing over 600 vessels in the village between the period of the American Revolution and the start of the Civil War in 1861. After the war, Essex continued to make steamboats during the 19th century and was a regular stop for sister steamships Hartford and Middletown.

Along with Essex, another community in Connecticut with a shipbuilding history is Haddam. Located on the east side of the Connecticut River, south of Hartford, Haddam has a rich history of sea captains, boat building, and commerce. The village's biggest wealth of history was found in the Knowles Landing community, home to many huge shipyards. In their heyday, these yards made six boats a year and big brigs and ships designed for ocean travel between intercontinental markets were their specialty. Hauling an average of 200 to 400 tons, they were frequently used for the lucrative West Indies trade and smaller sloops and schooners were utilized to transport rum from the local distilleries to New York City and the shoreline.

Hence, historians claimed that the first recorded large ship to be constructed on the Connecticut River was the snow (In sailing, a square rigged vessel with two masts, complemented by a trysail-mast stepped immediately behind the main mast) named "Mercury" built in East Haddam in 1751 to 1752. After it was built, 30,000 feet of lumber was loaded onto the "Mercury" at New London, Conn., on July 1752 and sailed to London, England about three weeks later.

In 1756, another snow named the "Augustin," with a weight of 180 tons, was constructed at the same yard in East Haddam. Then soon after these huge ships made in Haddam navigated the Connecticut, shipyards sprung up everywhere along the river. During that era, historians and researchers indicate that East Haddam was one of the largest shipbuilding ports in America and boats made in that town were seen in almost every port in the world. Yet in addition to shipbuilding in Haddam during the 1700s, commerce to and from the community consisted of lumber and farm products.

In addition to Haddam, another significant, historic community situated on the mouth of the Connecticut River worth mentioning is Old Saybrook. Although Old Saybrook was always a small town, it has a good trading history that kept it economically sound. In fact, in the 18th and 19th centuries, Saybrook depended on river trade and it became a key center for central trade and for transshipment from riverboats to oceanliners.

Its main harbor was Worth Cove, which before 1871, was a much deeper harbor than it is today. During the 1700s and 1800s, vessels sailing to and from Saybrook visited South America, Africa, and Europe. However, the main trade for ships sailing out of Old Saybrook was with the West Indies and along the U.S. eastern seaboard.

Another historic and significant town on the Connecticut River is Wethersfield, Connecticut. Due to its prime location on the river, Wethersfield initially established itself as a commercial center on the river since the 1600s. And that is when early trade at Wethersfield included exchanging wood products like shingles for greatly needed goods such as tools, clothes, and seeds from Boston, Mass.

Early regional trade was important at Wethersfield but soon after that trading with the West Indies became a top priority for the community and its economy. The West Indies trade was all about seeds, tobacco, horses, cattle, and other goods that were shipped from Wethersfield to the Caribbean. Returning ships to this Connecticut town and other nearby communities on the Connecticut River received salt, sugar, tea, and coffee.

Moreover, trade ships transporting commerce in and out of Wethersfield and vessels hauling commodities and other goods were made, owned, and operated by Wethersfield residents. In fact, during the 1600s and 1700s, Wethersfield was the main supply depot to the whole Connecticut River Valley. And in 1741, the well-known, 100-ton, Connecticut sloop-of-war called "Defence" was constructed in Wethersfield.

Another town on the Connecticut River worth mentioning is Rocky Hill, Conn. In the 1700s, Rocky Hill played a crucial role in Connecticut River commerce. The town also oversaw some of the busiest shipyards on the river. During the 18th century, yards in Rocky Hill were so financially sound back then that they were contracted to make the U.S. Navy's first ships in the 1770s.

Shipbuilders at Rocky Hill were at the summit of a major industry during the 18th century. At that time thousands of ships traveled the seas, rivers, and canals, an enormous network of trade. Sailors traveled up to six months to barter merchandise along the Atlantic seaboard and then they packed their vessels with salt, corn, rum, and onion.

Yet in addition to towns in Connecticut on the Connecticut River which built riverboats and were active in trade, shipbuilding and trade in communities outside of Connecticut on the river and in general also contributed to the local and national economy.

In fact by the 1850s, many shipyards along the Connecticut River manufactured shallow-draft boats used in cotton trade in the Gulf of Mexico and other areas. Shipbuilding on the Connecticut was also one of the biggest industries in the 1700s and 1800s.

Specifically between 1848 and 1881, about 24 boats were constructed across the Connecticut River in the Goodspeed Shipyard located in Boston, Mass. And over the years there were approximately 42 shipyards in business between Saybrook, Conn. and Springfield, Mass. During the early times these shipyards in Saybrook and Springfield made small coastal boats, sloops, and schooners that were utilized to haul granite, cobble and brownstone from the Connecticut River Valley to New York City.

Then by the late 1800s, boatyards on the Connecticut River joined forces in the lower valley where they started constructing 700 to 1,000-ton vessels. These heavy-duty, sturdy ships called packet boats were used for the cotton packet trade along the Connecticut River and in the European packet trade.

In addition to boats departing from Connecticut that contributed to national and overseas trade during the 19th-century, shipyards on the Connecticut made boats that sailed out of the New York Harbor. From 1850 to 1860, shipyards on the Connecticut River furnished 22 clipper ships (boats made to carry cargo) to the Port of New York and these vessels would sail from New York City.

Digressing to the period of the American Revolutionary War (1775 to 1783), shippers based at the Connecticut River were basically forced to trade with the Dutch, Spanish and French in order to maintain their profits. And although trade ships (sailing and steam vessels) on the Connecticut and other U.S. rivers did well financially during the 1700s and 1800s, by the close of the 19th century freight railroads put almost all sailboats and steamships out of business; it was the end of an era.

Chapter 3

History of Hudson River Boats with U.S. Waterborne Transportation, Travel and Trade

The Hudson River has a very long history of sailboats that navigated this waterway for hundreds of years. There are a variety of sailing vessels but one of the most famous, historic ones is The Half Moon. Built in 1608, The Half Moon was the name of the ship in which Henry Hudson discovered the river in 1609 that now bears his name. Hudson steered an 85-foot schooner (a square-rigged, three-mast wooden sailing boat).

In addition to Hudson's voyages, the state of New York also has a long history of ferries servicing the region. One service in particular, the Rhinecliff and Kingston Ferry Company, began to operate a ferry across the Hudson between the City of Kingston in Ulster County, N.Y. and Rhinecliff, a village in Dutchess County, N.Y.

For more than 200 years, the Rhinecliff and Kingston Ferry Co. operated on the Hudson. During the 1600s and 1700s, this ferry and other ferryboats were powered by sails and oars and initially transported livestock and other commerce across the river. Years later, the boats were driven by horses and sometime after 1851, steam power replaced the horses.

However, during the period of World War II, service on the ferry line was not consistent and in 1944, it ceased operations for the next two years between Kingston and Rhinecliff, N.Y. Yet the Kingston-Rhinecliff Ferry resumed operations in 1946 until 1957 when the Kingston-Rhinecliff Bridge opened, which replaced the need for ferries in the region.

Yet in addition to ferry service between Rhinecliff and Kingston, specifically from the 1700s until the early 1800s, sailing boats, specifically sloops (single-mast sailing vessels), were used mostly to transport passengers and goods on the Hudson River. Sloops that supported trade in the Hudson River Valley also impacted the development of our nation as a whole.

The era (18th century to early 19th century) of sloop commerce on the Hudson River is when these wooden sailboats used this waterway to ship between Albany, New York and New York City, the two principal business centers on the Hudson. Speaking of two, back then two famous, working sloops of the Hudson River were the Clearwater and Nancy. In 1794, the Clearwater, which was 44 feet long and weighed 35 tons, was manufactured in Albany, New York. The Clearwater hauled freight making frequent stops to New York City and Albany. The Nancy was about half the size of Clearwater but was another hard-working sloop that made many stops in New York and Albany. From the mid to late 1700s, Albany had an advantage over other cities geographically and was the center of trade with western territories and Native Americans. The sloops were designed for bulky cargo such as cement, ice, bluestone, etc. they often hauled and traded through Albany and other states northeast of New York State. Hence, flour, fur, timber and peas came from trade on the Hudson River with Native Americans. And by the 1790s, sloops were regularly transporting fish, mail, and passengers.

By 1810, 206 sloops sailed the Hudson and these vessels were constructed in almost every Hudson River town. Among the boats registered between 1789 and 1867, Nyack in Rockland County, New York built 170, followed by Marlboro in Ulster County with 112 and Albany with 106. In the lower Hudson Valley, Mount Pleasant made 76 and Peekskill constructed 62.

Early sloops on the Hudson were called freight sloops, merchant sloops or market boats. These boats had no regular time of departure or destination. They sailed when and where goods were available to be carried. Cargoes on Hudson River sloops varied. For instance, produce like timber, grain, flour, hay, and furs were transported downriver to the cities. However, manufactured materials and imports such as hardware, tobacco, oil, cloth, and sugar sailed upriver. The peak of the sloop era was around 1830 when on a summer day, one hundred of those vessels could be spotted on the Tappan Zee between Tarrytown and Nyack, New York. Also during the 1800s, Newburgh, N.Y. became a main hub of commerce in the mid-Hudson as sailing sloops from Newburgh engaged in international trade.

Although cargo was a chief component of sloop commerce on the Hudson, passenger travel was an equally important business for sloop owners and operators. Sloops were made to provide passenger travel as these boats provided fast and comfortable transportation up and down the river. In fact, some sloops transported 25 to 30 passengers a trip.

In the early 19th-century, demand for passenger travel skyrocketed and competition between sloops became stiff, making passenger-only vessels and expanding the size of cabins. In fact, one boat named the Illinois, had a cabin stretching half the length of the boat. Moreover, the speed of sloops is very important to passenger and cargo commerce. If tide, wind, and weather were favorable, the trip from New York City to Albany could be made in 20 hours. Derived from Dutch and British sloops, the single-mast Hudson River sloop continued to dominate the transportation business on the Hudson River for decades, even after the arrival of steamships.

Indeed steam-powered boats arrived on the Hudson River thanks to inventor Robert Fulton. In 1807, Fulton tested his North River Steamboat, the first steam-powered vessel on the Hudson and began commercial operation up and down the river a few months later. In 1808, Fulton's steamship started to make weekly trips on Wednesdays going south to Catskill, New York and on Sundays, he headed north to Catskill. Then in 1811, another inventor, John Stevens, designed his twin screw-driven steamboat, Little Juliana, on the Hudson. In that same year, Little Juliana operated as the first steam-powered ferry between Hoboken, New Jersey and New York City.

After Fulton's historic steamboat invention and trips, the Hudson had a total of three steamers in 1814. These vessels took about 32 hours to travel from New York City to Albany, New York. In addition to Fulton's vessels, one popular steamship that served the Hudson for decades was called Norwich.

Built in 1836, Norwich, also known as the Ice King, operated on the river for 74 years. Constructed for the New York and Norwich Steamboat Company for service on the Long Island Sound, the Norwich stayed on that route for the next seven years before she started navigating the Hudson in 1843.

During 1843, Norwich was placed on the Rondout, N.Y.-New York City route for passengers and cargo. Then five years later, she was transformed into a towboat. In 1848, Norwich became the "Ice King" in that she weighed 346 tons, was 160 feet long and had a depth of nine feet, which enabled her to break through the heaviest ice on the river.

Norwich was the last steamship that operated when winter and early spring arrived each year on the river. For many years, she would free many steamers and barges from the icy Hudson until finally in 1923, the Ice King was dismantled and no longer served the Hudson River.

Digressing to passenger ferries operating during the 19th century, the "Air Line" ferryboat was one of the first of the "walking beam kind" ferries ever erected in the U.S. Built as a wooden hull vessel at Philadelphia in 1857, the ferry, "Air Line," was originally constructed for the Air Line Railroad Company of Pennsylvania. The boat was also unique in that it only had one bow instead of the customary two which back then was the rule for ferryboats. The "Air Line" served passengers between the New York State towns of Saugerties and Tivoli on the Hudson for almost 58 years and continued its service for the public until 1915.

Getting back to steamships, it was not until the 1860s when steamboat travel on the Hudson River peaked and passenger and cargo transportation provided by steamers continued to regularly serve towns up and down the river until the late 1920s.

And when it comes to passenger steamboat travel, the Hudson River Day Line comes to mind. Known as the most famous Hudson River steamboat line throughout the U.S. and the world, Hudson River Day Line focused on "passenger only" travel and it achieved a cachet of elegance that freight ships could not boast.

By the close of the 1902 season, Hudson River Day Line, the biggest operator of day steamboats on the Hudson, acquired and operated a large, passenger side-wheeler named Mary Powell. Built in 1861 at a shipyard in Jersey City, N.J. and also known as the "Queen of the Hudson," Mary Powell sailed the Hudson for 55 years. She was also one of the fastest, most attractive, and dependable steamboats of her time.

Mary Powell had a cruising speed of about 24 mph and was designed as a day steamer strictly for the carrying of passengers on the Hudson. For her entire career, Mary Powell's schedule was to leave Kingston, N.Y. early in the morning and make stops in New York State towns that included Poughkeepsie, Milton, Newburgh, and Cornwall, arriving at the lower Manhattan pier in the late morning. On her return, she would leave New York at 3:30 p.m. and arrive back in Kingston in the early evening. The typical time of operation was from May to late September.

But over time, the role of Mary Powell changed. After decades of transporting passengers on her Kingston-New York City run, the Day Line from 1914 to 1917 continued to start and end her seasons on her Kingston to New York City run but during the peak of the seasons she was used for charter trips (New York City to Bear Mountain and back) and on special trips to Albany.

Finally on September 5, 1917, she sailed on her old route and it was Mary Powell's last trip. By January 1920, Mary Powell was placed on her old winter dock on Rondout Creek, N.Y. and was sold for scrapping.

In addition to Mary Powell, other large, popular passenger steamers were operated by Hudson River Day Line. These steam-powered vessels include the names of Daniel Drew, Aremenia, Chauncey Vibbard, Albany, New York, the Hendrick Hudson, Robert Fulton, Washington Irving, Alexander Hamilton, and the Peter Stuyvesant.

In 1863, steamers Daniel Drew and Aremenia began to operate on the Hudson River on the Albany to New York City run on the same schedule as a single line. Also both vessels traveled at a speed of 22 miles an hour and completed their trip in 7 hours. This combined operation marked the start of the Hudson River Day Line.

A year later (1864), another steamer, Chauncey Vibbard, was launched. Chauncey was a 265 foot-long, passenger side-wheel steamboat with a top speed of almost 30 m.p.h. that paired with Daniel Drew on the Hudson to provide regular steamboat service between New York City and Albany.

And as one navigated upriver, the other traveled downriver and officials with Hudson River Day Line claimed it took 9 hours for the boats to finish the trip between Albany and New York City, with Poughkeepsie being the halfway point.

After Chauncey Vibbard was introduced to passenger travel on the Hudson, a side-wheeler steamer called Albany was announced by the Hudson River Day Line in 1880. Albany operated from 1880 to 1930 on the Hudson River and was touted as a fast boat that could match or surpass the speed of steamer Mary Powell.

Albany was a 300-foot long riverboat that featured huge cabins and displayed paintings by famous artists to her guests. Albany could accommodate up to 1,500 passengers and her regular trip consisted of the Albany/New York City run.

Along with Albany came another passenger steamer named New York that was introduced into service in 1887. Like Albany, New York could transport up to 1,500 passengers and was assigned to the New York City-Albany route.

New York was a first-class ship and its interior décor showcased many fine paintings that gained Hudson River Day Line steamers the reputation of being "floating galleries of art."

After the late 1800s passed by and riverboats Albany and New York made their marks in history, the 20th century later represented another period of continued heyday years for steamships on the Hudson.

By 1906, a new steamboat for the new century was introduced to New Yorkers and America. This was a steel hull, side-wheel steamer, the Hendrick Hudson, launched by Hudson River Day Line as the first "million dollar" ship to ply the river.

Built by Marvel Shipbuilding Company based in Newburgh, N.Y. in 1906 at a cost of almost $1 million, she was over 400 feet long and could carry up to 5,500 passengers. Soon after it was ready to go, Henry Hudson would continue to serve passengers on the New York City to Albany run until 1948.

Just three years passed (1909) and steamship Robert Fulton was introduced to provide passenger service on the Hudson River Line. Robert Fulton came to life just in time for the Hudson-Fulton Celebration as it replaced steamboat New York that burned at Newburgh, N.Y. in 1908.

In observance of the celebration, three steamers of the Day Line: Hendrick Hudson, Robert Fulton, and Albany led the first division of the large naval parade marking the centennial of steam navigation and the 300-year anniversary of Henry Hudson's voyage up the Hudson River.

Following Fulton was steamer Washington Irving, the next passenger riverboat to appear on the Hudson. A 416-foot long, side-wheel day boat, Washington Irving was launched in 1912 by the New York Shipbuilding Company at Camden, New Jersey.

Being a very large ship, she could transport almost 6,000 passengers and was constructed only for day boat service between New York City and Albany. Washington Irving was also the biggest and most exquisitely furnished steamer in the world.

Then as the years rolled on the Day Line introduced another steamer called Alexander Hamilton in 1924. This vessel was the last side-wheel steamship constructed for the Hudson River Day Line.

Built at Bethlehem Steel Corporation in Sparrows Point, Maryland, Alexander Hamilton was 338 feet long and at a cruising speed of 21 mph could carry up to 3,700 passengers and a crew of 50. When she first operated, she transported passengers along the Hudson River between New York City and Albany, N.Y. In later years Alexander Hamilton's trip was shortened between New York City and Poughkeepsie.

Finally in 1966, she was owned by Circle Line Sightseeing, Inc. who operated her under the name, Day Line. Sailing from Pier 81 by West 41st Street in Manhattan, Alexander Hamilton made the sightseeing trip up to New York State's Bear Mountain State Park and West Point, then returned downriver with the passengers back to Manhattan; she remained in service until 1971.

Another steam riverboat operated by the Hudson River Day Line was the Peter Stuyvesant, which was launched in 1927 from the yard of Pusey and Jones Company at Wilmington, Delaware.

Moreover, she was the first propeller-operated ship managed by the Day Line and was designed for passenger excursion purposes, replacing the Day Line's Washington Irving that was sunk by a tug-oil barge in New York Harbor the previous year (1926). Peter Stuyvesant, the last of the large ships made for the Hudson River Day Line, ran from 1927 to 1962 on the Hudson from New York City to Albany.

Digressing to its popularity according to historians and researchers, riverboats operating under the Hudson River Day Line were and remain the most popular passenger vessels on the Hudson. But another significant passenger boat that I want to focus on is the riverboat Binghamton.

Between 1904 and 1906, Virginia-based Newport News Shipbuilding erected the Binghamton. Made of steel, she was 230 feet long and 62 feet wide.

Binghamton also established a long track record of transporting commuter passengers across the Hudson. From 1905 until 1967, she carried commuters across the river between lower Manhattan and Hoboken, N.J. And unlike ferries before her launching, Binghamton was permitted to load and unload passengers from two decks. Furthermore, she had two double-ended wheelhouses so that it could cross the Hudson River and return without turning around.

As the years passed and more subway trains transported people under the Hudson, its steamer service ended in 1967. But fortunately in 1976, she was converted into a restaurant called Binghamton's while its new home was relocated to a pier in Edgewater, N.J.

However in 2007, the restaurant closed and now the last double-ended steam ferryboat on the Hudson is an eyesore sitting on the bottom of the river across the Hudson from Grant's Tomb in Manhattan.

In addition to Binghamton, other ferries provided service on the Hudson via the Manhattan/New Jersey trips. One popular steamship line company in particular that operated riverboats from New York City to New Jersey was the Englewood-Dyckman Company.

Beginning in 1915 and continuing decades after that, ferryboats operated by Englewood-Dyckman Co. transported passengers and automobiles from Manhattan Island to the Palisades Beaches in New Jersey across the Hudson River. Then later during the early 1930s, ferry and beach use was at its prime but when the George Washington Bridge opened in 1931, ferries experienced stiff competition from cars traveling on highways. Ferry usage soon plummeted from that time onward and finally the ferry company ceased operations in 1942.

Day Boat *Albany* passing *Old Storm King* on the Hudson River
Courtesy of the Historical Society of Rockland County
in New City, New York

Str. "Washington Irving" of the Hudson River Day Line.

Washington Irving on the Hudson River
Courtesy of the Historical Society of Rockland County
in New City, New York

The Tivoli-Saugerties Ferry (also called the *Air Line*)
on the Hudson River

Courtesy of the Saugerties Public Library
in Saugerties, New York

Cornell towboat *A. B. Valentine*, ca. 1880s, on the Hudson River. The *Valentine* featured the large side paddlewheels typical of most of the towing steamers and passenger steamers of the 19th century (1800s) on the Hudson.

Courtesy of the Donald C. Ringwald Collection,
Hudson River Maritime Museum in Kingston, New York

The Ferryboat *Air Line* had a cut-out metal silhouette of
an American Indian atop its multi-sided pilot house
Courtesy of the Donald C. Ringwald Collection,
Hudson River Maritime Museum in Kingston, New York

Steamer *Emeline* at dock on lower Hudson River

Courtesy of the Donald C. Ringwald Collection,
Hudson River Maritime Museum in Kingston, New York

Steamer *City of Albany* passing pair of schooners and a sloop
Courtesy of the Donald C. Ringwald Collection,
Hudson River Maritime Museum in Kingston, New York

Unidentified sloop with ferry boat in background,
New York Harbor on the Hudson River near New York City

Courtesy of the Hudson River Maritime Museum
Collection in Kingston, New York

The Hudson River Day Line Steamship *Albany* with the Hudson River Day Line Steamship *Mary Powell* directly behind her on the Hudson River. The *Mary Powell*, built in 1861, also known as the "Queen of the Hudson," transported passengers on the Hudson River for fifty-five years.

Courtesy of the Historical Society of Rockland County
in New City, New York

Chapter 4

History of Hudson River's Shipbuilding/Trade Towns

From the 1600s to the 1800s, towns along the Hudson River were significant to the shipbuilding industry and tour economy on a local, national, and international level. Some of these communities that I will focus on include the New York State communities of Nyack, Newburgh, Greenpoint (part of Brooklyn, N.Y.), Albany, Poughkeepsie, and Rondout Creek.

For instance during the 19th century, the Dutch settled in Nyack and many of them were farmers. These same Dutch farmers also owned a sloop to transport their produce to markets in New York City.

In the early 1800s, farmers along the banks of Nyack discovered that outcropping of red sandstone provided them with an additional "cash crop" for which there was a ready demand in the City of New York. The quarry business along the Hudson in Nyack thrived and between 1810 and 1840 there were 31 quarries near Upper Nyack.

Moreover, Hudson River sloops were enlarged and improved. The sloops provided a critical transportation link on a local, national, and international scope as these vessels transported passengers, produce, freight, and stone. Stimulated by the demand to carry stone and brick, Nyack constructed many boatyards and by far became the biggest manufacturer of sloops along the Hudson. Also due to passenger demand in the 19th century, Nyack was a home to many ferry landings.

Like Nyack, Newburgh, New York was a shipbuilding town on the Hudson River. In the late 1700s, Newburgh rapidly became the first significant shipping point on the west bank of the Hudson north of New York City because of its superb harbor, and its natural outlet for trade in America before canals and railroads became popular.

Shipbuilding continued to carry on in Newburgh and soon ships from this town in New York State entered into the West Indies and Liverpool trade. By 1800, Newburgh became a principal hub of commerce in the mid-Hudson. Sailing sloops from Newburgh engaged in international trade and steamships stopped on the way between Albany and Manhattan.

During the 20th century, industries in Newburgh such as clothing factories, brickyards, and shipyards were flourishing. During World War I, shipyards were widely expanded and many cargo ships were made in the area. Some of these cargo vessels were named after Hudson River towns such as Newburgh, Poughkeepsie, Firthcliffe, Irvington, and Peekskill.

Greenpoint, which is part of Brooklyn in New York City, is another important and historic ship oriented community. From 1850 to 1865 (end of Civil War), Greenpoint was one of the major shipbuilding areas in the world. And for nearly fifty years after the Civil War, this area in Brooklyn near the Hudson River continued to make ships and was quickly populated by many shipbuilders and their families.

In fact, the shipyards in Greenpoint built some of the biggest wooden craft ever manufactured in the U.S., including clipper ships, three mast schooners, and smaller wooden vessels. Greenpoint also created iron warships that helped the North win the Civil War.

As early as the 1830s, the development of shipbuilding in Greenpoint coincided with a huge demand for sailing ships. Trade with China created an enormous need for ships and New York City then became America's biggest center for shipyards.

After 1840, big shipping lines demanded more iron hulled ships; but nonetheless, Greenpoint's waterfront was completely turned into an array of shipyards by 1855 and the area continued to build wooden vessels until the late 1800s.

Albany, the capital of New York State, is another city on the Hudson that is significant to our national and international economy. As early as the 17th century, Albany began serving as a port on the river when in 1614 the Dutch initially established a trading post there. Then about ten years later, the Dutch built a fort in Albany where goods like sugar, timber and rum were transported over from Europe and the West Indies.

In 1642, ferry service started in Albany and the city was developed for commerce on both sides of the Hudson River. In 1664, trade did well in Albany and that is when three docks were built there to accommodate more ship traffic. During the early 1700s, for long haul and lesser vessels to be able to cross the river and conduct nearby trading, Albany's commerce down the Hudson River and mainly with New York City had taken over the Hudson's business by assembling and maintaining its own sloops. And overall economically, Albany continued to be an important city regarding trade and transportation on the Hudson well into the 17th and 18th centuries.

By the 19th century, Albany became a full-fledged transportation center and the city remained a contributor to waterborne travel and trade on the Hudson River until the 20th century. In 1931, the Albany Basin opened, which provided moorings for numerous sloops, steamships, and canal boats and in 1932, the Port of Albany opened for business. Today, the Port of Albany is home to forest and grain products and customers all over the world depend on the port's handling of salt, molasses, iron, steel, and other products.

In addition to Albany and the other river towns that I mentioned, another historic one on the Hudson is Poughkeepsie, also known as the Queen City of the Hudson.

Poughkeepsie is a significant city in the state of New York because of its numerous geographic features, its proximity to the Hudson River, its central location between Albany and New York City, and its coves. For 100 years (1776 to 1876), Poughkeepsie was known as the Shipyard Point where the Revolutionary War Shipyards and many different kinds of ships were constructed along the city's waterfront.

Speaking of ships, in 1793, ferry service began between Highland, N.Y. and Poughkeepsie as a sail and rowboat operation. In 1800, a sailboat named Brig Caroline was launched and Poughkeepsie started to serve as New York State's second seaport. In 1819, a two-horse-powered "Team Ferry Boat" started passenger service to and from the city and 80 years later in 1899, a side-wheel ferry named the Brinkerhoff, began operation between Poughkeepsie and Highland, N.Y. The Brinkerhoff made her final trip in December 1941 when its service ceased operation.

With its closeness to the river, water traffic and trade made Poughkeepsie a fast growing port and town. Poughkeepsie is located in the middle of two large New York cities and over the years, became a sensible stop for many travelers and traders. Also its coves provided a place for vessels to anchor and gave people easy access inland. Not surprisingly, the name, Poughkeepsie, was originally derived from an American Indian word and actually means "safe harbor."

One more community of the Hudson River that I wish to mention is Rondout Creek, New York located about 100 miles north of New York City.

The "canal-constructing period" of the early nineteenth century tremendously impacted the village of Rondout when the Delaware and Hudson Canal (D and H Canal), which opened in 1828, chose Rondout as the end of the canal and beginning location for river traffic headed to New York City.

Thanks to the D and H Canal, all commodities flowed through Rondout and as steamship traffic increased during the 1820s and 1830s, Rondout rose to become the main Hudson River deep-water port in the Hudson Valley and became the center of maritime activity between New York City and Albany. Then in the 1840s and 1850s, the "bluestone" business bloomed in Rondout and the stone was prepared in Rondout, which met the demand in towns across the U.S. During this period, shipyards capable of manufacturing boats ranging from ice and coal barges to sloops, schooners, and steamships moored the riverbanks of Rondout Creek.

Yet besides bluestones, the Cornell Steamboat Company was based in Rondout, where many vessels were berthed and repaired, and some boats were made there. Also in the mid-1800s, Cornell Steamboat Company constructed a side-wheeler steamer to ply the route from Rondout to New York City. She was named after Thomas Cornell, who founded the company in 1837 and then more than fifty years later in 1900, Cornell Steamboat Co. had given up the passenger boat business and focused on towing vessels and tugboats.

Between 1830 and 1900, only a few harbors in the United States were as busy as Rondout Creek; however, growth of Rondout stopped in 1899 when the Delaware and Hudson Canal closed. Then in 1932, just three decades after Rondout was the principal port of the Mid-Hudson Valley, only a pocketful of industrial companies remained in business in that small village on the Hudson River.

But in addition to the harbor in Rondout, N.Y., the history of trade conducted at New York Harbor in New York City at the mouth of the Hudson River was also significant to the development and economies in the region, throughout the United States, and in other countries abroad.

In the early 1800s, the Port of New York had the same trading volume as the other main ports, such as Baltimore, Philadelphia and Boston.

During the early 19th century, Boston was the busiest port in the U.S. due to its established marine industry, while New York was still adjusting to trading goods originating from the colonies after being the only major city controlled by the British throughout the Revolutionary War.

In 1820, Boston and New York each exported over $10 million of goods but by 1840, New York Harbor handled more passengers and cargo than all other harbors in the nation combined. The reason for New York's arrival was the "cotton triangle," a newly created trade between the Southern states, New York and Europe that made New York's port the consolidation and distribution center for the entire United States.

Cotton and tobacco from Southern farmers were shipped by the Port of Baltimore to New York and ships returned to the Southeast transporting manufactured goods from Northern states. There were two reasons how New York became a hub for the cotton triangle: development in marine technology and the city's geographic advantages over other ports. With the Erie Canal's completion in 1825, the Port of New York benefited from steamships by giving farmers and traders access to New York markets, which served as a consolidation point for other East Coast and European markets. For example, wheat grown in Indiana could travel by steamship across the Great Lakes, through the Erie Canal, and down the Hudson River to New York City, where it could be exported to England.

Chapter 5

History of Delaware River Boats with U.S. Waterborne Transportation, Travel and Trade

As early as the 1600s, the Delaware River was a critical waterway for transportation and trade as European settlers began to navigate the river themselves. Back then, canoes or small wooden boats started to transport goods on the Delaware.

By the 18th century, the Delaware River became home to many timber rafts, ferryboats, and Durham Boats. In the mid-1700s, a timber raft normally consisted of logs or lumber stabled together with cross poles across the raft's 25-foot width, making a watercraft up to 200 feet long. Steering oars were made out of 35-foot-long logs and a 6-foot-long rudder board was bolted to the boat.

During the time of the timber raft, the shipbuilding industry in Philadelphia looked to the Upper Delaware Valley for tall trees with which to make spars and masts for the timber rafts but transporting them was not easy. Navigation was a big challenge and since most rafting was done in rapid, high water during the spring, exact anticipation of quickly approaching hazards was required. Rocky river rapids were dangerous to rafters and their biggest fear came as they approached the narrow spaces between bridge abutments. Besides problems with guiding it on the river, a raft's only accommodations were short logs serving as seats and a tarp covering an oil lamp, food, and rubber rain jackets. Moreover, timber rafts were only operated during the day.

In addition to timber rafts, ferryboats were used at that period to cross the Delaware River. During the mid-1700s, a ferry was rectangular and came with a flat-bottomed, shallow-draft box acting like a floating deck onto which horse-drawn wagons, carriages or cars could be driven. While their dimensions differed as widely as the number of ferryboats in existence, most were at least a few yards longer than a horse hitched to a wagon. Yet other ferries were long enough to haul two automobiles and passengers. Ferryboats were rowed, poled, or guided with ropes or cables stretched across the river on which two dollies ran, attached by rope to each end of the ferry's body.

In fact, two ferries across the Delaware River in the Trenton, New Jersey area date from the late 17th century – the Yardley Ferry and the Trenton or Middle Ferry. Two more included the Upper and Lower Ferries that were added later in the 18th century. In 1683, the Yardley Ferry, four miles above the falls of the Delaware, was established and it operated into the mid-1830s. And according what local historians claimed, the Trenton or Middle Ferry may have been operating as early as 1675; this ferryboat crossed the Delaware River just below the falls.

Then later in the 1770s, the Trenton Ferry had to compete with another ferry line on the Delaware when Lamberton, New Jersey began to expand from a fishing village into Trenton's port and became a river town. This ferry was called the Lamberton or Lower Ferry. For many years it competed with the Trenton Ferry and from 1776 to 1781, provided service as the "Continental Ferry" where U.S. servicemen could cross the Delaware River at reduced rates.

A third ferry, the Upper Ferry, also began operating on the Delaware during the time of the Revolutionary War. Crossing close to where the Calhoun Street Bridge crosses the river today, this ferry was used around the period of the Battles of Trenton in the winter of 1776-77. All three Trenton ferries (Upper, Middle and Lower) competed for river crossing business for the next 25 years or so. However, their significance rapidly faded in 1806 after the first Trenton, N.J.-Morrisville, P.A. Bridge opened for business.

Besides the ferryboat, another vessel introduced on the Delaware River in the mid-18th century was called a Durham Boat. The boat's namesake, Robert Durham, started to manufacture the boats along the Delaware River's Pennsylvania coastline in upper Bucks County, P.A. north of Philadelphia. The purpose of the Durham Boat was to transport iron ore from places upriver back to Durham's Iron Furnace in Bucks County. The boat also hauled cannonballs from Durham's furnace to Philadelphia and it ferried General George Washington's army across the Delaware River before his 1776 Christmas attack on the Hessians at Trenton, New Jersey.

Back then many people described Durham Boats as trough-like. The boats were 40 to 60 feet long with an eight-foot beam and their flat-bottom design allowed them to draw less than two feet of water when completely loaded. Durham Boats could haul up to 18 tons downriver, but just a few tons upriver. And just like most vessels, the era of Durham Boats came close to the end. After the 1860s, these vessels were rarely seen on the Delaware River, a lot of their business was shifted to canals and railroads.

During the 19th century, steamboats were popular vessels seen navigating the Delaware River. Although steamers were invented in the 18th century and sailing boats were still around, the peak period of steamships operating on the Delaware was during the 1800s.

Some famous steamers that were made and operated out of Philadelphia along the Delaware River in the late 19th century include the SS Pennsylvania, SS Ohio, SS Indiana, and SS Illinois.

The first of four sister steamships launched in Philadelphia was the SS Pennsylvania. In August 1872, William Cramp and Sons in Philadelphia constructed SS Pennsylvania and this passenger and cargo iron steamship was the first vessel of the American Steamship Company of Philadelphia. With a length of 355 feet, a depth of 43 feet, and a capacity of 3,016 tons, this steamer was one of the biggest ships ever made in America.

SS Pennsylvania departed Philadelphia with 56 passengers for her maiden trip on May 22, 1873; she returned from Liverpool, England on June 23. Her career as a ship lasted decades and SS Pennsylvania operated from the Delaware River for the next 44 years until 1918 when it was destroyed in a fire in Chile.

The SS Ohio was the second big iron steamship constructed by William Cramp and Sons in Philadelphia. Ohio was 343 feet long, had a depth of 32 feet, and a beam of 43 feet. She was launched in 1872 and its first voyage took place in August 1873 on the Philadelphia-Liverpool route.

The Ohio traveled at a speed of up to 11 knots and could transport 46 first class passengers, 132 second class people and up to 789 steerage passengers. She continued operating the Philadelphia-Liverpool trip for the next 22 years but unfortunately, the SS Ohio was wrecked off the coast of British Columbia on August 26, 1909.

Like SS Ohio, the third iron steamer, SS Indiana, was made by Philadelphia-based William Cramp and Sons Company and operated by the American Steamship Company in Philadelphia. Also like SS Ohio, she was 343 long with a depth of 32 feet and a beam of 43 feet. Indiana's passenger capacity and speed was also the same as her sister ship, Ohio.

Furthermore, the SS Indiana traveled the same way (Philadelphia to Liverpool) as the Ohio and its first voyage was in October 1873. Indiana also continued to operate on the same route for the next 24 years. Subsequent to the Spanish-American War (April 1898 – August 1898), another steamship company, the Pacific Mail Steamship Company (incorporated in 1848), acquired Indiana and after decades of dependable passenger and cargo service, she was grounded off the coast of Mexico in April 1909.

The last of the Pennsylvania-class steamboats manufactured by William Cramp and Sons and operated by the American Steamship Company was the SS Illinois. The length, beam, depth, and speed of Illinois were identical with that of steamers SS Indiana and SS Ohio. Its first trip was in January 1874 and the route of Indiana was also like its sister ships and it continued the Philadelphia-Liverpool run until 1886.

But what set the SS Illinois apart from its sister passenger/cargo ships that I mentioned was that it had a major refit in 1891 with the installation of a triple-expansion steam motor (new and smaller engine that provided more cargo space) that replaced her original compound steam engine.

Seven years later, SS Illinois deviated from her normal route and in March 1898 began navigating from Philadelphia to San Francisco, California. Then just a month later in April 1898, she was sold to the U.S. Navy to serve in the Spanish-American War.

Steamship *Burlington* on the Delaware River. In 1915, it sank on the Pennsylvania side of the Delaware River across from Bordentown, New Jersey.

Courtesy of the Bucks County Historical Society
in Doylestown, Pennsylvania

Chapter 6

History of Delaware River's Shipbuilding/Trade Towns

Just like significant river towns that lie along the Connecticut and Hudson rivers, the Delaware River has its fair share of historic communities along its shores that are very important to the area's economy, our U.S. economy, and our global economy.

Some river towns on the Delaware worth mentioning that are important to the economic lifeline of the surrounding communities include the New Jersey towns of Trenton, Bordentown, Burlington, Camden, and three towns in Pennsylvania definitely worth mentioning, which are Bristol, Chester, and Philadelphia.

The first two towns that played a positive role with the Delaware River region's economy that I will focus on are cities that lie next to each other on the river are Trenton and Bordentown.

During the 18th century, Trenton became a port on the Delaware River for shipping products and grain traveling between Philadelphia and New York City. The city was also a main stopping point on the stagecoach line the two bigger cities. Then a ferry, chartered in 1727, connected Trenton with Philadelphia, finishing the transportation circle.

Moving forward to the 19th century, Trenton sloops played a significant role in rendering the British blockade at New York City and Philadelphia during the War of 1812 (1812-15). During the war, these sloops carried an array of military supplies from Philadelphia to Trenton where they were loaded on wagons and transported to New Brunswick, N.J., then carried forward to New York.

Bordentown, Trenton's neighboring community, also contributed positively to the Delaware River area. In the 17th century, Bordentown was a small city settled by Quakers on the Delaware located about 45 miles upriver from Philadelphia. Yet despite its size, it was in an ideal location on the Delaware; and soon it became a colonial water transportation hub.

Founded in 1682, the city became a river transportation hub indeed and in 1717, Joseph Borden, a farmer that the town was named after, launched packet boats (small boats designed for transporting domestic mail, freight and passengers in North American rivers, canals and European countries) from Philadelphia to Bordentown where passengers would stop to rest and then go on Borden's stagecoach line to Perth Amboy, N.J., where they made their connection to New York City. In addition to passenger travel, Bordentown became a booming city of trade in the late 1700s.

Later in the 19th century, specifically from 1810 to 1820, there were many steamships navigating the Delaware between Philadelphia and Bordentown. Also during the 1800s, Bordentown blossomed into a thriving shipping and manufacturing center; local industries there consisted of a canning factory, ironworks, and a shipyard.

Two other New Jersey shipbuilding towns south of Trenton and Bordentown that are significant to the economy of the Delaware River are Burlington and Camden.

In fact, Burlington was a well-established river crossing even before English Quakers landed in New Jersey and other parts of America in 1677. Burlington was where early Dutch settlers operated a rope ferry to convey passengers and wagons between the town and Bristol, P.A.

Meantime, Burlington became a major colonial port and maintained a brisk trade with Great Britain, Ireland, Europe, and the West Indies. And in 1698, the city's first shipyard opened and shipbuilding became one of Burlington's important economic activities. Although in the 1700s, the city's importance as a port declined with the growth of Philadelphia's, boatyards in Burlington continued to make a variety of smaller sailing vessels including skiffs (shallow, flat-bottomed open boats with sharp bows and square sterns), sloops, and racing yachts.

Then by the 19th century, boating became a popular recreational activity for Burlington's wealthy population. Moreover, since 1788, the world's first steam powered boat started to make regular trips between Burlington and Philadelphia and passenger service from Burlington continued into the early 20th century.

Going back to the Colonial Era, in addition to Burlington's significance on the Delaware River and to the boating industry during that period, the first European settlers made their home along the banks and towns of the Delaware River where the Dutch and Swedish vied for control of the local fur trade.

Moving forward, the next river town I will focus on is Camden. In the 1700s and 1800s, a steady increase of ferryboats and steamships transported freight and passengers back and forth on Camden-Philadelphia trips. And it is no wonder that for more than 150 years, Camden served as a secondary transportation hub for the Philadelphia area.

Moreover, from 1899 to 1967, this city in South Jersey became home to the New York Shipbuilding Corporation (then the biggest shipyard in the world).

New York Shipbuilding was at its peak during World War II (1939-45) and naval vessels made there include cruiser USS Indianapolis and the aircraft carrier USS Kitty Hawk. Also during WWII, RCA Victor, Inc., a major company based in Camden, provided electronics for warships made in the Greater Philadelphia Region. Then two decades later in 1962, the first commercial nuclear-powered ship, the NS Savannah, was launched in Camden.

Moving ahead as I cross the Delaware to Pennsylvania, two important river towns there that boosted the local and national economy on that section of the Delaware River include Bristol and Philadelphia.

First there's Bristol, a community near Philadelphia, that definitely made maritime history in Bucks County, P.A. in that according to historians, during the 1700s, the first ferry in Bucks County to cross the Delaware between New Jersey and Pennsylvania operated out of Bristol.

Also in the 18th and 19th centuries, sea-going vessels could sail to Bristol and that was a critical element in creating the area's shipbuilding industry. In addition, many ferryboats and steamships during that period navigated the Delaware between Bristol and Burlington, N.J.

Digressing to shipbuilding, for most of the city's history, Bristol was the only location in Pennsylvania above Philadelphia where a shipbuilding industry was established. As for ferries and steamers operating out of Bristol on the Delaware River, both services continued until 1931 when the Burlington-Bristol Bridge was erected.

In addition to Bristol, there's Chester, Pennsylvania, a city that sits on the western bank of the Delaware River between Philadelphia and Wilmington, Delaware. Like Bristol, Chester is a riverboat town and its history of boatbuilding goes back to 1859 when Thomas Reaney, a shipbuilder from Philadelphia, founded his own shipyard, named Reaney, Son and Archbold, in Chester. Over the next 11 years, Reaney constructed 6 naval combatants, 20 cargo ships, 17 tugs and 8 smaller vessels, averaging almost five boats a year. However, his business began to fall following the Civil War and he was forced to sell the yard to John Roach of New

York, who renamed it The Delaware River Iron Shipbuilding and Engine Works.

By 1887, the shipyard Roach owned in Chester was the biggest one in America but John Roach died. His older son, John Baker Roach, took over the yard but the company closed when John Baker Roach died in 1908.

In 1913, the idle shipyard was purchased by Charles Jack, then a retired U.S. Navy Captain, who reopened the yard as Chester Shipbuilding Company. But World War I started and Jack did not have the money needed to re-equip the yard so in 1917 he sold it to Averell Harriman's American Ship and Commerce Corporation, which renamed the yard Merchant Shipbuilding Company. Nevertheless, the new owners soon decided that the shipyard in Chester was not suitable for mass production as they originally thought and then they set up a new yard upriver, in the Bristol section of Philadelphia.

But despite what happened to the yard, the shipyard in Chester remained operating until 1924 when it permanently closed. The shipyard once occupied 23 acres along about 1,200 feet of Chester's industrial riverfront, stretching from Pennell Street to Fulton Street along West Front Street, just north of today's Commodore Barry Bridge. During its prime years, the Chester Boatyard had ten building berths and six wet berths, although those berths are not there today. After the yard closed shop in 1924, the site was redeveloped as a Ford assembly plant.

Finally, the third shipbuilding community along the Delaware River worth mentioning is Philadelphia, a huge, significant town on the Delaware River. Without a doubt, Philadelphia during the Colonial Period (1607 – 1776) made a tremendous impact on the area's economy and our nation's economy.

In the Philadelphia region alone, demand for merchant ships, specifically scows (large, flat-bottomed boats used for carrying loads, often towed by tugboats), sloops (sailing vessels having a single mast with a mainsail), schooners (ships with two or more masts, rigged fore and aft), and brigs (sailing boats with two masts and square sails) together made a sudden, huge push for shipbuilding along the Delaware Riverfront.

By 1720 there were about twelve shipyards in the City of Philadelphia and its surrounding riverfront area manufactured wooden sailing ships weighing up to 300 tons! Thanks to the shipyards, the City of Brotherly Love became a rich city and in 1750, Philadelphia with its ship builders, carpenters, and huge number of trees had replaced Boston, M.A. as America's major colonial shipbuilding center.

Perhaps in some ways the Colonial Era represented the golden age of shipbuilding along the Delaware River in Philadelphia. Moreover, between 1727 and 1766, Philadelphia's shipyards manufactured 737 vessels. By the time of the American Revolution, the city was the dominant seaport in the United States. In fact, New York City did not surpass Philadelphia until the early 1800s.

And also by the early 19th century is when shipyards in Philadelphia on the Delaware River suffered setbacks due to the War of 1812. That was the period when numerous, privately operated yards ceased to make ships or boats. Yet despite the setbacks, a number of 19th century economic and individual developments revived shipbuilding on the Delaware River before the start of the Civil War (1861-65).

The first shipyard to recover was the Philadelphia Navy Yard along the city's riverfront area. This yard led to the construction of the biggest wooden warship ever made for the U.S. Navy, the 120-gun Pennsylvania, launched in 1837. Meanwhile, in the years before the Civil War, the William Cramp and Sons Ship and Engine Building Company began to assemble wooden sloops, tugs, schooners, and passenger ships, many powered by steam.

After the Civil War, Philadelphia suffered a shipbuilding depression but years later it started to bounce back again by World War I (1914 -18) when William Cramp's Company became the most important shipbuilding operation on the Delaware River.

Yet it wasn't until World War II that represented the most important era for shipbuilding in the Philadelphia and Delaware River Region when the Philadelphia Navy Yard employed 50,000 workers. The yard built two large battleships, New Jersey and Wisconsin, and over fifty warships including torpedo-equipped vessels and fast aircraft carriers.

A commerce port on the Delaware River in
Philadelphia, Pennsylvania circa 1850

Courtesy of the Independence Seaport Museum
in Philadelphia, Pennsylvania

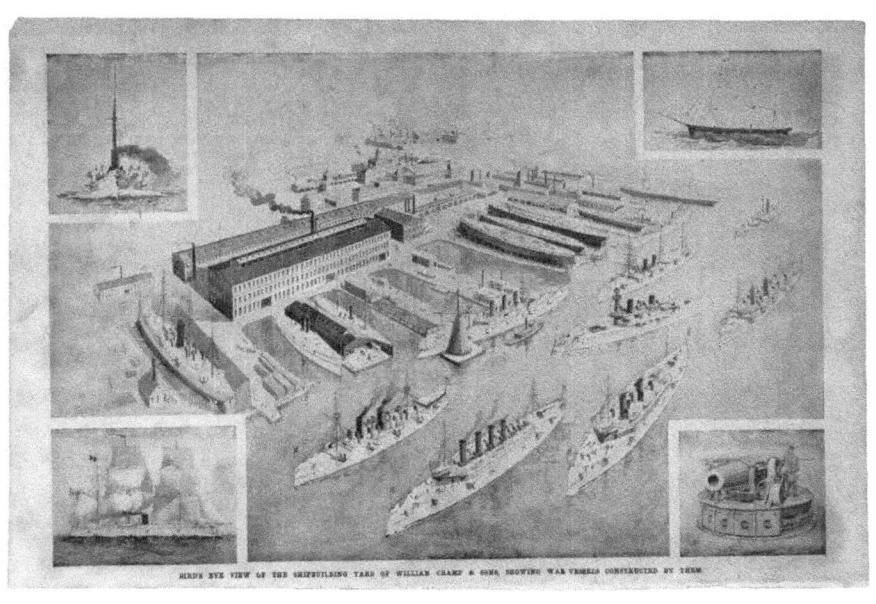

The shipbuilding yard of William Cramp and Sons

Courtesy of the Independence Seaport Museum
in Philadelphia, Pennsylvania

Philadelphia ferry and wharf about 1850.
Courtesy of the Independence Seaport Museum
in Philadelphia, Pennsylvania

Trenton Marine Terminal (opened in 1937) in Trenton, New Jersey with Steamer *Tannentels* at the dock on the Delaware River.
Courtesy of the Trenton Historical Society
in Trenton, New Jersey

Chapter 7

Canals That Improved Navigation for Vessels Transporting Commodities and Passengers on Connecticut, Hudson, and Delaware Rivers

For thousands of years canals have been constructed for drainage, irrigation and later transportation. Commodities could be transported more efficiently on water than on horseback or in wagons. Engineers designed canals where no suitable water existed and in the early 1700s, European settlers saw the need for canals in the U.S. but our country couldn't afford to build canals until the early 1800s.

It was then in the 19th century, that canals were made to help speed up travel, especially commercially, from one part of the river to another. These man-made waterways had been used successfully in Europe and Asia for centuries, as a way to provide more efficient, faster, and cheaper transportation.

More canals were constructed in the 20th century and are comprised of dams and locks. Navigation dams are constructed on rivers to hold back water and create deeper navigation pools. Dams make it necessary for riverboats to make a series of locks to step up or down the river from one water level to another and safely bypass the dam. Moreover, canals were and some still are crucial waterways that enhance navigation of river vessel traffic on U.S. waterways including the Connecticut, Hudson, and Delaware Rivers.

Regarding the Connecticut River, canals were constructed there between 1791 and 1828 at different sections of the river to overcome the different rapids and falls along its path. Canals built for the Connecticut resolved the navigation problem specifically in transportation by flat boats and steamships.

During the nineteenth century, one important canal of the Connecticut River was Enfield Falls Canal, which was constructed in 1829 to circumvent the shallows at Enfield Falls (or Enfield Rapids) on the Connecticut between Hartford, Conn. and Springfield, Mass. The canal was 5 ¼ miles long, had a vertical drop of 32 feet and is located along the west side of the river. Enfield Falls Canal is situated next to the towns of Suffield and Windsor Locks in Hartford County, Connecticut and Windsor Locks are named after the series of locks on the canal. The locks admitted vessels up to 90 feet long and 20 feet wide and the canal was unique among canals of that era in that it was designed with structural reinforcement to facilitate steam tugboat traffic.

Once the canal was opened, vessels were able to haul much larger loads, and the upcoming steamship services were introduced using newly designed boats capable of passing through the lock chambers. However, by 1844 the Hartford and Springfield Railroad began operating and navigation on the Connecticut River slowly dwindled.

Today, Enfield Falls Canal is listed in the National Register of Historic Places, but closed to navigation. The Ahlstrom Corporation, which has a manufacturing complex next to the canal, now privately owns it. The locks themselves still exist but have not been used since the 1970s. Presently, most of the towpath is open for cycling and hiking at the Windsor Locks Canal State Park Trail, a public recreational area paralleling the Connecticut River for 4.5 miles between Suffield and Windsor Locks, Connecticut.

One canal significant to the region is the South Hadley Canal along the Connecticut River in South Hadley, Massachusetts. This canal opened for commercial traffic in 1795 and it was unique in that many other canals used locks but South Hadley Canal was built with an inclined plane that was utilized for transporting 20-foot by 60-foot flatboats over the falls. And in

1826, the Barnet, first steam vessel to navigate the Connecticut River, passed through this canal on its way to Vermont.

Another canal worth mentioning was the one chartered for the Connecticut River at Bellow Falls, Vermont in 1791. However, due to the gigantic fall of the Connecticut River (52 feet), it took ten years to construct the nine locks and dam before the first vessel passed through the canal in 1802. Boats continued to go through Bellow Falls Canal until 1849 as railroad traffic began to rise and boat traffic tremendously declined.

Like Bellow Falls, another canal, the Turner Falls Canal, originally opened for business in 1802. Erected in 1798, Turner Falls had ten locks, was along the Connecticut River in Montague, Massachusetts, and supported regular freight boat traffic from Long Island Sound to Bellow Falls, Vermont.

The Canal at Turner Falls operated profitably for the next 30 years and in 1826 was even briefly part of a bigger system from Boston to the Hudson River. However in 1856, it was closed to navigation because of stiff competition from the railroads. But in 1869, it was rebuilt to provide waterpower for existing and future planning mills.

Then after 25 years passed from the time when Bellow Falls and Turner Falls opened, and the Canal at Windsor Locks, Connecticut opened for business in 1828. Erected by the Connecticut River Company, this six-mile-long canal was at the southern part of the Connecticut River. This canal also made navigation of the river more feasible and freighting cheaper.

Like the Connecticut River, canals truly benefited the Hudson River's freight vessel transportation system. One canal in particular was the Erie Canal. In 1823, the first ships entered the Hudson River from the Erie Canal and by 1825 the entire Erie Canal was finished.

New York Governor DeWitt Clinton officially opened the Erie Canal in 1826 when he traveled in the packet boat, Seneca Chief, along the canal where he began his voyage from Buffalo, New York and completed the 363-mile trip nine days later in New York City. From that point on, freight ship traffic continued to boom from the Erie Canal to the Hudson River until 1931.

However in 1931, a railroad joining Albany and Schenectady, New York was completed and that slowed down boat traffic. But in 1836, a program for enlarging the Erie Canal to a 70-foot length and a 7-foot depth was initiated.

But it was not until 1847 that work resumed on the Erie Canal Enlargement Program. Meanwhile, at the same period in which officials of New York State were encouraging the development of canals they were also encouraging the development of railroads, competition for waterborne transportation.

In addition to the Erie Canal, another popular canal, the Delaware and Hudson Canal (D and H Canal), also benefited transportation on the Hudson River.

In the early 1800s, most canals were financed by U.S. states but the D and H Canal was the first canal in our nation constructed as a private enterprise. In 1828, the Delaware and Hudson Canal opened its completed 108-mile length and after it was finished, the canal was four feet deep, 32 feet wide, contained 137 bridges, 108 locks, and 26 basins, dams, and reservoirs. The D and H Canal was a transportation system between the coalfields of northeastern Pennsylvania and trade on the Hudson River.

Initially the canal provided navigation for vessels that weighed 10 to 35 tons and after 15 years, the D and H Canal accommodated boats that weighed 136 tons that would go directly from the canal to markets up and down the Hudson River. However, after many years of being the conduit for trade and travel on the Hudson River, the Delaware and Hudson Canal finally closed in 1899 when the mode of preferred transportation changed from ships to trains. Businesses then discovered it was more feasible to ship its coal by train and as demand for year-round products increased, canals became obsolete and the D and H Canal became the Delaware and Hudson Railroad.

Later in the 20th century, another historic canal benefiting the flow of riverboat traffic on the Hudson River is the Troy Lock and Dam located at Troy, New York. Over a century ago, the Hudson River and other navigation channels in America were kept at specific depths so that boats can safely transport their materials along the river. To maintain this certain depth, it was mandated in the early 1900s that a system of locks and dams be built on rivers.

One good example of an effective lock and dam system is Troy Lock and Dam, which opened in 1915. Like the Erie Canal and D and H Canal, the Troy Lock and Dam greatly enhanced navigation on the Hudson. In fact, the Lock is one of the oldest ones in the U.S. and is over 100 years old.

Today, the Troy Lock operates each year from May 1 to November 30 and still provides great financial and recreational support to the area serving as a conduit to the New York State Canal System.

Originally, the U.S. Army Corps of Engineers erected the Troy Lock and Dam so it could improve navigation between the Hudson River and the New York Canal System, which included the Erie Canal. The Army Corps has operated the lock and dam ever since it was opened.

Over the years and even now the Troy Lock and Dam is beneficial to shippers. For instance, one gallon of fuel will move a ton of cargo 576 miles by barge. In addition to commerce shipping, the lock supports tour boats, yachts, and different types of recreational vessels.

The canal system at Troy, N.Y. also benefits the town and people on its shoreline. Folks can bike on its parallel path, fish on it, paddle with canoes and kayaks on it, and take dinner cruises.

Yet in addition to canal systems on the Connecticut River and Hudson River used by captains of ships for commercial and recreational navigational reasons, canals constructed in the 19th century also benefited vessels on the Delaware River.

So it's no surprise that in 1832, the Delaware Canal was erected. The canal ran from one side of Pennsylvania to another, from Bristol to Easton, where it connected with the Lehigh Canal. The chief purpose of these two waterways was to carry anthracite coal from the northeastern Pennsylvania coal regions to towns on the eastern seaboard.

During the most productive years just before the start of the Civil War, more than 3,000 mule-drawn boats traveled up and down this route, transporting over 1 million tons of coal a year. Smaller quantities of goods such as produce, building stone, lime, and timber were also transported.

Over the course of its length of 60 miles, the Delaware Canal dropped 165 feet through about 23 locks. The canal was about 60 feet wide and was five feet deep where ten aqueducts carried the waterway over small valleys and streams.

However, starting in the 1840s, railroads competed with riverboats for cargo contracts as revenues and traffic from canals in Pennsylvania plummeted. By 1858, the Delaware Canal was sold to private operators and from 1866 to 1931 the Delaware Canal was operated by the Lehigh Coal and Navigation Company that also owned the Lehigh Canal.

In 1931, 40 miles of the Delaware Canal was deeded to the Commonwealth of Pennsylvania and was named Roosevelt State Park. In 1940, the Commonwealth acquired the entire 60-mile canal and in 1989, the park was renamed Delaware Canal State

Park. The importance of the Delaware Canal was recognized in 1978, when it became a National Historic Landmark. Today, it is preserved as the last towpath canal in the U.S. capable of being fully- restored and watered.

In addition to the Delaware Canal, another important canal that boosted the cargo ship traffic industry in the Delaware River Region is the Delaware and Raritan Canal (D and R Canal). The canal, which opened in 1834, is located in central New Jersey and represents the connection between the Delaware River and the Raritan River. The canal was opened to become an efficient and reliable means of transportation of cargo between Philadelphia and New York City. William Penn, founder of Pennsylvania, originally suggested the idea of the canal in the 1690s. This canal would shorten the voyage from Philadelphia to New York City by 100 miles and relieve the need for vessels to venture into the Atlantic Ocean.

The main section of the D and R Canal runs from Bordentown, New Jersey on the Delaware to New Brunswick, New Jersey on the Raritan. A feeder canal section (feeds water into the main canal) stretches 22 miles northward from Trenton, N.J. upriver along the east coast of the Delaware to Bull's Island near Frenchtown, New Jersey. The entire length of the total canal system was about 66 miles. The main section was 44 miles long, 75 feet wide and 8 feet deep. The feeder canal portion was 22 miles long, 60 feet wide and 6 feet deep.

During the 1860s and 1870s, the D and R Canal was regularly used to transport coal from Pennsylvania to New York City. However, over the years, the importance of the canal waned as trains were used to perform, more quickly, the same function as canals but nonetheless, it stayed in business until 1932. Years later, the portion between two New Jersey towns, Trenton and Bordentown, was filled for different road and rail projects, leaving the feeder waters to supply the main canal from Trenton north to New Brunswick, N.J.

Today, a section of the main D and R Canal in Trenton has been covered over (the water still flows underneath) by the Trenton Freeway and is inaccessible to public use. The portion of the canal that provided access to the Delaware River in Bordentown is also abandoned.

Another smaller canal that was important for transportation and trade on the Delaware River was called the Chesapeake and Delaware Canal (C and D Canal). Although it was just 14-miles long, the C and D Canal crossed the northern Delaware/Maryland peninsula, and its eastern mouth is at Reedy Point, Delaware, on the Delaware River, with its western mouth at Chesapeake City, Maryland, on Chesapeake Bay. The canal's name reflects the name of the two bodies of water that it connects.

Made in the 1820s, C and D Canal opened in 1829 and became one of the few fully ocean-level shipping canals in the world. With 10 feet of water depth and four locks, the canal carried barges and sailing boats that were towed by mules and horses. In 1919, the U.S. government bought the canal and over the years, the U.S. Army Corps of Engineers expanded it many times. During the 1920s, C and D Canal was deepened to make a sea level facility with a 12 feet deep, 90 feet wide, channel with no locks, which was finished in 1927. From 1935 to 1938, the canal channel was deepened to 27 feet of water depth and widened to 250 feet.

By the mid 1970s, more deepening/widening projects increased the channel depth to 35 feet of water depth, with the channel width increased to 450 feet that was sufficient for two-way traffic for most oceangoing vessels. The C and D Canal provided a shortcut passageway of around 300 miles for boat traffic between the Port of Baltimore, Maryland and the northeastern U.S. cities and Europe.

Furthermore, the C and D Canal is the only main commercial canal in America that is still in use, among those that were constructed during the heyday of canal building in the early

1800s. The canal also has bicycle and hiking trails along the coastline of most of the canal's length.

Chester Hadlyme Ferry on the Connecticut River
Photo taken by Al Braden

Glastonbury Ferry on the Connecticut River
Photo taken by Al Braden

Becky Thatcher Cruise Boat on the
Connecticut River near Chester, Connecticut

Photo taken by Al Braden

Chapter 8

Today's Boats Navigating the Connecticut, Hudson, and Delaware Rivers

The Connecticut River today is a busy waterway regarding recreational and commercial boat traffic. As for pleasure boaters, common ways to cruise the Connecticut are by canoe, kayak, sailboat and small powerboat. Canoeing is popular on the upper river as the lower river is all flat water and is navigable by large vessels up to Hartford, Connecticut.

In addition, cruises on the Connecticut are now available to the public and I will mention a few of them. For example, the Connecticut River Museum in Essex, Connecticut offers river cruises on the Connecticut aboard the historic vessel, Onrust. The Connecticut River Museum claims Onrust is a replica of pioneer Adriaen Block's vessel, which was launched in the mid-1600s and it's one of the first sailing ships constructed in the New World. The museum also stated that Onrust was America's first yacht and the first vessel ever to sail up the Connecticut River. Cruises aboard the Onrust on the Connecticut are now available for the public from Thursdays to Mondays. The Onrust is a vessel that serves to educate visitors about the era of exploration, the fur trade, and our Colonial Period. The boat is also available for exploration while docked at the Connecticut River Museum.

Another ferryboat in service on the Connecticut River today is called the Rocky Hill – Glastonbury Ferry that dates back to 1655. The Connecticut River Museum and Connecticut Department of Transportation claim that this ferry is America's oldest continuously operating ferry service that crosses the Connecticut River between two towns in Connecticut, Rocky Hill and Glastonbury.

Today, the vessel is an open flatboat named the "Hollister III" that provides a direct link between Rocky Hill and Glastonbury at Route 160. Its season of operation is currently from April 1 to November 30, seven days a week. Motorists traveling between parts of Glastonbury and Rocky Hill can reduce almost 8 miles (one-way) off their trip when they use the ferry. The boat also benefits cyclists because it serves as the only crossing between Hartford, Conn. and Middletown, Conn.

Yet besides what the Onrust and Rocky Hill – Glastonbury boats provide for passengers and the public, there is the educational Winter/Wildlife Eagle Cruise that operates on the Connecticut River from February 3 through March 18.

And once visitors board the Connecticut River Expedition's 64-foot RiverQuest, during the winter when temperatures are below freezing, travelers can see Bald Eagles from as far north as Canada, go to the open waters of the Connecticut River (these eagles also fly to the Hudson River and Upper Delaware River) to fish, perch, and nest.

In addition to pleasure watercraft navigating the river, commercial traffic on the Lower Connecticut River is bustling, mostly from tugboats and barges. Barges and other big commercial vessels stay in the channel while local ship captains recommend that recreational boaters stay off the river at night due to heavy commercial traffic.

Today, the Hudson River is also a busy river accommodating recreation and commercial vessels. Regarding recreational boats, the Hudson now offers the public sightseeing cruises and some of these sightseeing ships include Hudson River Cruises, Circle Line Cruises, Newburgh Landing, and Albany.

Located in Kingston, New York, about two hours north of Manhattan, Hudson River Cruises offers music cruises, dinner party cruises, and family-oriented cruises. All cruises are two hours long and depart from the Rondout Landing in Kingston. Another cruise for folks staying in Manhattan that want to get a taste of the historic river is Circle Line Cruises. Circle Line provides three-hour cruises that circumnavigate the island, traversing the Hudson River, East River and the Battery.

More river cruises up the Hudson launch from other river towns such as Newburgh Landing and Albany, both located in New York State. Passengers can now take a cruise on the Hudson from Newburgh Landing on the ship named "Pride of the Hudson." Pride of the Hudson offers two-hour sightseeing tours that feature a main salon and outdoor decks. Sights along the way include West Point and Storm King Mountain (located along the west bank of the river and forms the northern gateway to Newburgh Bay).

Meanwhile, Dutch Apple Cruises offers two-hour sightseeing tours, dinner cruises, and private charters that depart from Albany, N.Y. This cruise has two enclosed decks equipped with heat and air conditioning, a dance floor, and offers passengers live entertainment. In addition to cruise vessels, many people operate sailboats, motorboats (including yachts), and kayaks for pleasure up and down the Hudson especially during the summer.

The Hudson is also a "working river" where each day people along its coastline and on boats will have no problem spotting gigantic commercial ships traveling in and out of New York Harbor in New York City. Every day from the Port of New York, container ships, barges, oil tanker vessels, other freight watercraft, and tugboats transport a variety of commerce downriver to the Atlantic Ocean and upriver to towns north of New York. Some of these cargo vessels are based out of the Hudson and are used as export ships while others come from all over the world to import us goods.

In 2016, pilots based out of the New York Harbor made over 10,000 trips aboard tankers with oil, orange juice and other goods. They also navigated bulk ships hauling salt, sand, and other cargo in and out of the port.

Regarding trade via Port of New York, statistics indicate that in 2016 the top trading partners by value with the port were China, Germany, India, Italy, Japan, United Kingdom (U.K.), France, South Korea, Israel, and the Netherlands. Also the harbor's top trading partners by volume (thousands of metric tons) were China, India, Italy, Germany, Brazil, France, Netherlands, South Korea, U.K. and Thailand.

As for 2016 imports for the New York Harbor, beverages, machinery, and soaps came from the U.K., carpets, furniture, and sugar arrived from Turkey, and beverages, plastics, and cocoa were shipped from Belgium. Some of the 2016 exports consisted of grains, aluminum, and waste paper sent to Vietnam, textiles, machinery, and base metals transported to Pakistan, and U.S. vehicles, chemical products, and machinery were shipped from the Port of New York to Ghana.

In addition to ship traffic and trade at the Port of New York, one more freight vessel worth mentioning is the Apollonia, a steel-hulled schooner, now plying on the Hudson. In an effort to bring back sail freight to the Hudson River, the Apollonia will soon haul freight on the Hudson.

The Apollonia is a 64-foot-long, 15-foot-wide schooner that was made in Baltimore, Maryland in 1946. Besides sails, the vessel has a diesel engine that helps it maneuver 20,000 pounds of cargo. Today, the crew is working with local businesses along the river to offer an option to moving products by truck.

But like how sail freight was during the 1700s and 1800s, the Apollonia won't be fast enough for perishable goods. However, the good news is the schooner works well for transporting heavy, shelf-stable products such as cider, beer and wine.

Of course just like the Connecticut and Hudson Rivers, the Delaware River now is another waterway that is constantly active with pleasure and commercial boats.

Some cruises on the Delaware include Albatross Marine Services, American Sailing Tours, Bucks County Riverboats, Liberty Belle, Riverboat Queen, Spirit of Philadelphia, and the RiverLink Ferry.

Albatross Marine provides a 28-foot Maine lobster boat for its cruises on the Delaware. A charter service for six passengers, it's available for fishing trips, bird watching, and river cruises. A second cruise is American Sailing Tours that features the Summer Wind vessel, the only steel-hulled Chinese schooner available for public sail in North America. It sails up to five times every day from the Philadelphia waterfront along the Delaware River, with 90-minute cruises available. In fact, one trip includes the History Sail, which is a tour of the history of Philadelphia and the Delaware River. Next there's Bucks County Riverboats; the Bucks County Riverboat Company operates out of Keller's Landing in Bucks County, Pennsylvania. Their 52-foot boat, the River Otter, can accommodate up to 76 passengers and offers catered lunches and dinners as well as hors d'oeuvre and cocktail cruises.

In addition to the River Otter, there's the Liberty Belle that is a 6-story Mississippi-style paddle-wheel riverboat with three enclosed decks and four outdoor decks. Once aboard the Liberty Belle, visitors can enjoy the Delaware like 19th century passengers but in more modern style, with music and dancing on the daily lunch and dinner cruises. Another cruise on the Delaware is on board the Riverboat Queen, which is a replica of a paddle wheeler moored at the Wilmington Riverfront in Delaware specializing in all-you-can-eat crab cruises and private charters. Its upper deck has an open-air dancing area and strolling view of the river and the lower deck provides travelers with and enclosed, climate-controlled experience.

Besides the Riverboat Queen, the Delaware has the Spirit of Philadelphia vessel that is one of the biggest Delaware River cruise ships which features three enclosed decks that can accommodate up to 550 passengers in cruise-style seating and a fourth deck that comes with outdoor patio seats for diners. The service offers two-hour trips throughout the day, including dinner, entertainment, and moonlight cruises. Finally, there is the RiverLink Ferry that currently navigates the Delaware. The RiverLink Ferry offers passengers cross-river transportation between the Camden, N.J. and Philadelphia, P.A. Waterfronts during the summer. This ferry provides daily transportation for visits to local water attractions and all major waterfront events on the New Jersey and Pennsylvania sides of the Delaware River.

Along with recreational vessels, the Delaware River, specifically the Lower Delaware River, is a main waterway for commercial ship traffic especially for huge watercraft dealing with trade. It is commonplace that workers unload cargo at different ports on the river from ships arriving from Singapore, Liberia, Bahamas, Hong Kong, Denmark, Panama, and the Netherlands. This cargo included automobiles from South Korea, goods from England, fertilizer from Algeria, paper products from Finland, crude oil from Texas, and fruit from Central and South American countries.

According to the Maritime Exchange for the Delaware River and Bay, around 400 ships carrying 6 million tons of cargo arrive annually. The Maritime Exchange also indicates that top Delaware ship imports are fruit from the Americas; containers from Europe and the Americas; petroleum from Europe, Canada and the U.S.; along with steel from Europe, Japan and Russia. Meanwhile, the leading U.S. exports coming from ports located on the Delaware River are gas and petroleum products, vehicles, and minerals.

One of today's cargo vessels by the Port of Camden
in Camden, New Jersey on the Delaware River

Photograph by Mike Mallon

A giant modern cargo ship that is along the Port of Wilmington in Wilmington, Delaware on the Delaware River

Photograph by Mike Mallon

A freighter ship navigating on the Hudson River near the Port of New York by New York City

Photograph by Mike Mallon

The *Circle Line*, a popular cruise vessel, that is transporting passengers on the Hudson River so they can see the skyline of New York City

Photograph by Mike Mallon

The *NY Waterway Ferry* that takes passengers on daily roundtrips from the Hudson River along Manhattan, New York to different destinations in New Jersey

Photograph by Mike Mallon

The *Ben Franklin*, a cruise/passenger vessel, plying on the Delaware River. It operates out of Penns Landing at Philadelphia, Pennsylvania.
Photograph by Mike Mallon

The passenger ferry, *Freedom*, passing the battleship *New Jersey* on the Delaware River at the Philadelphia, Pennsylvania/ Camden, New Jersey waterfront area.

Photograph by Mike Mallon

Author's Summary

The three rivers (Connecticut, Hudson, and Delaware) I researched and wrote about all have vessels that plied their waterways and each contributed greatly to the founding and economic development of their regions' riverfront towns. These three streams also have a history of trade, travel, and transportation (geared for both recreation and commercial purposes) that boosts local economies in Connecticut, New York, New Jersey, Pennsylvania, Delaware, and Maryland.

Recreational watercraft attracts visitors from the Northeast region, across the country, and overseas. Furthermore, the fleet of cargo and other commercial ships boosts the economies of regional ports. And when container ships, freighter ships, oil tankers, tugboats, barges, and other workhorse vessels navigating up and down the Connecticut River, Hudson River, and Delaware River engage in trade, this ignites the economy at the local, national and international levels.

Of course other waterways in the U.S. such as the Missouri, Mississippi, Illinois and Ohio Rivers have pleasure watercraft and commercial ships that contribute largely towards travel and transportation throughout our country. These rivers are also important to our nation's foundation and development and boost local, national, and international trade which jumpstarts economies at the local, national and international levels. However, I chose to learn more about the Connecticut, Hudson, and Delaware Rivers and write about these waterways because several times I have visited these streams and have a personal connection with these rivers, especially the Hudson and Delaware.

And although the purpose of my book focuses on today's and yesteryear's ships that cruise and used to navigate the

Connecticut, Hudson, and Delaware Rivers benefiting trade, travel, and transportation (locally, nationally, and internationally), these three streams are home to many of the same fishes that swim and migrate under their waters.

Some fish throughout the year that live, spawn, and/or visit the Connecticut River, Hudson River, and Delaware River include the American shad, bass, trout, pike, catfish, walleye, river herring, carp, Atlantic sturgeon, grouper, bluefish, and perch.

Getting back to the surfaces of the Connecticut River, Hudson River, and Delaware River, all three waterways are crucial to the local maritime industry and economies in the region, the U.S., and throughout the world. The history of boats (pleasure and commercial) that cruised the above three waterways also played an important part in the foundation and development of trade, travel, and transportation in America. Furthermore, the history of shipbuilding towns, ports, and canals located on and near the three rivers boosted vessel traffic (passengers and cargo) in local riverfront towns, which positively impacted the local and the U.S. economies.

Moreover, for centuries, ships engaged in trade that plied the Connecticut, Hudson, and Delaware Rivers exported and imported a vast, variety of goods to towns throughout America and the world. Craft engaged in waterborne trade created jobs, uplifted revenues for businesses in local river towns, and jumpstarted our national and international economy.

Today, you will still see recreational and commercial vessels traveling on the Connecticut, Hudson, and Delaware Rivers. Nowadays, many people travel aboard cruise ships and often navigate these rivers on kayaks, canoes, and powerboats. Of course, you may not see as many commercial ships on the waters like in the past because back in the 1800s, freight trains became competitors of sailboats and steamships and gradually took away much of their business. Railroads move faster than boats and now haul a lot of cargo and other goods to different destinations that boats used to transport. However, shipping by boat on the above three rivers will never disappear as long as vessels are in safe, operating condition, harbors remain in business, and the Connecticut River, Hudson River, and Delaware River keep flowing!

About the Author

John Bernardo is the published author of six books. John's latest book was a non-fiction one that focused on passenger and cargo vessels which navigated and still navigate the Connecticut, Hudson, and Delaware Rivers. These same vessels are major and positive contributors to the history, development and future of America's waterborne transportation, travel and trade industries.

Bernardo became a freelance journalist in 1988 and is the published author of over 500 articles (some were published in magazines and the rest in newspapers).

John's interests include visiting different rivers, nature centers, museums, and railroad museums. Born and raised in Westchester County, New York, he currently resides in Miami, Florida with his wife, Agustina, and two daughters, Michelle and Melissa.

www.ingramcontent.com/pod-product-compliance
Lightning Source LLC
Chambersburg PA
CBHW050844160426
43192CB00011B/2142